pages of my life

Poems of My Journey

Majoniwasa Utishala
formerly known as
Elayne Anderson

DREAM HOUSE PUBLISHING
http://www.dreamhousepublishing.biz

pages of my life

Poems of My Journey

Majoniwasa Utishala
formerly known as
Elayne Anderson

Other book by author

Computer Love

Finally I got it done!!!

This collection is especially dedicated to William H. Taylor, III - - -

Bill I hate you for leaving me but I love you for loving me - - -

Sam thanks for sharing.

I will love you forever

Finally I got it done!!!

Surprise! Most of you knew about the novella, not many about the poetry. Thanks to family and friends for your continued prayers and encouragement. Dr. Sando this is only the beginning. My children, Sonia, Najla, Geika & Jabari: DO NOT ... I repeat DO NOT throw my papers away read them carefully, they may be a work in progress.

Finally I got it done!!!

All praises to Allah!!!

Table of Contents

About the Author

I was born in San Francisco, California. In the fourth grade, I wrote my first short story which disappeared with my fourth grade teacher. I attended San Francisco City College where my first poem was published in the college newspaper. While in northern California, I also attended San Francisco State University where I met William (Bill) H. Taylor, III, the author of four books of poetry, who until his death was a continuing source of encouragement and inspiration.

After becoming frustrated with life in San Francisco, I moved to Los Angeles, California. I attended California State University of Los Angeles and Compton Community College. I graduated from Pacific Union College with a Bachelor's degree in Nursing. I have a Master's Degree in English literature in progress at California State University at Dominguez Hills.

Currently I live in Compton, California and work full time as a registered nurse.

Poetry, as Bill always said, not only "seeks analysis and connection but also illustrates and examines roles played, choices made and consequences laid to rest "

I thank you for turning these pages.

Majoniwasa Utishala

pages of my life

Poems of My Journey

Voice of the Negro

Four hundred years ago
my soul was taken
I became a Voice
the voice of the Negro
crying to America

I want to be a man
who loves
who hopes
who belongs

I want to love
my parents
my family
my life
but the capacity to love was taken from me

I want to hope for a tomorrow
of love
of peace
of happiness
but the reasons to hope were taken from me

I want a homeland
a country
a heritage
a language of my own

I am not a voice
I am not a Negro
I am an African

Stripped
I was taken away
from my family
from my country
from my heritage

Stripped
I was taken to
a country of meanness
of cruelty
of much hate
and confusion

I want to go home
I do not belong

I am tired
oh
so very tired
of being abused
of being misused
of being less than second class

I want a change
I demand a change
There WILL be a change

No longer will I be a voice
I will be a man
a black man
a strong black man

I will be a happy man
who loves
who hopes
who belongs

A CHANGE IS COMING!

I will no longer be the voice of the Negro
I will no longer cry to America
I will belong to a nation
a nation of Africans

(1968)

Africa . . . . . Africans

I think of Africa today
of all the changes
of all the problems
of all the people
of all their ways

I dream of Africa at night
of the heartbreak
of the disappointment
of the hurt and bodily harm

As I dream of Africa at night
I know somewhere, somehow
things are not quite right

I think
I dream
I wonder

what if
why not
how could they
why didn't they

I think
I dream
I wonder

what if
my people
had been left alone to live their own life

why not
leave us alone
let us go our way

how could they
come in
take over
take out
drain
exploit
use
misuse
abuse

why didn't they
leave us alone

let us live
let us love
let us die

you made us over
I liked the way were

Big
Black
Beautiful
Deep
Dark

You made me over

I was big but kind
I was black but sincere
I was beautiful but trusting
I was deep but shallow
I was dark but rich

You made me over

what
why
how

you made me a beast
much like your self
no longer am I a man
I am animal of a sort
BEASTLY

you made my blackness blacker
you didn't understand me
you made me a man
much like yourself
WILD

you made beautiful me ugly
my manner
my tradition
my lifestyle
you made me ugly
much like yourself
FRIGHTENING

I was deep but not deep enough
you dug deeper
you drained me
you made me an animal
much like yourself
CLAWING

I was dark, you made me darker
the tales you told
the lies you told
you made me an animal
much like yourself
SLY

why?

I didn't deserve

I was happy
I was content
I was wise

you took my heart
you took my soul
you took my love

I can't give anymore
I am broken
I won't love anymore
you may take it away

If I hate ....I am happy
only because you made me
this way

Deep
Dark
Big
Black
Beautiful

naked
stripped
I lay open to the world

you did this to me
you made me this way

don't laugh at me
don't ridicule me
don't help or try to understand me

you took my clothing
you took my heritage
you took my shame

I lay open
exposed to the world

Africa.... African

Deep
Dark
Big
Black
Beautiful

Freedom

people power
hush
Black power
settle down

Scream and shout
free the mind
FREE THE MIND!

Free minds are needed
free minds claim freedom
free men have free minds

free the mind
FREE THE MIND!

I beg of you
let my mind go free
you can't I know
'cause to free my mind
is
to
free
me!

Peace

I'm tired of living

but

I don't want to die

until I discover

a

way

to live

in peace

with

my

brother

My Dream

*My dream is
of a day
when I
will know of
nothing
but
happiness*

*My dream is
of a day
when the world
will know of
nothing
but
peace*

*My dream is
of a day
when my black brothers
will know of
nothing
but
love
for each other*

Democracy

Democracy is so damn good
America has to go to other countries
killing her people and theirs too

Democracy is so damn good
America has to take a people
tie them down
prop open their mouth
and feed it to them

Democracy is so damn good
America hasn't the time to treat all HER people equally

Her time is spent devising ways
for others to live

America
we don't like hypocrites
America
what you have is not what we need
America
if this is the democratic way
we do not need your democracy

HOPE

*I am here
to live
to love
to die*

*Before I leave
I will live
I will love
I will die*

*I only hope
I will have lived a life
I
love
dying
for*

NEEDER

I cry
because
I
need
love

I
need
YOUR
love

love me?

You can't
I know
because
you have
people
at home
your home
your people
that
you love
more
than
me!

Either . . . Or

The world today is in opposition with itself
There is no middle ground
everything
is
Either......OR
Either big or little
Either straight or crooked
Either hot or cold
Either up or down
Either square or round
Either right or wrong
Either good or bad
Either urban or rural
Either rich or poor
Either light or dark
Either left or right
Either city or state
Either state or nation
Either liberal or conservative
Either black or white
Either freedman or slave

The world today is at opposition with itself
There is no middle ground
everything
is
Either ......Or
today
I'm looking for a place
where
everything
is
Neither......Nor

Majoniwasa Utishala

WORDS, WORDS, WORDS

hey you
please
stop trying to tell me
what
I
am

'cause there is no word
in your language
that crazy
mixed up
undefinable
tongue of yours
that you can use
to tell me
what
I
am

Why must you try
to dictate
to me
what
I
am
how I should live
how I should love

What is your problem
white boy / white man
whatever you want
to call yourself

I really don't give a good damn
what you
want to
call you
or
me

No!
What you say doesn't mean
anything to me
yours is a sorry way
of
expressing yourself
of
defining you

So
Why must you use your
words
to try so hard to define me
to tell me
what
I
am

*or
to tell me
what
I
am
not*

*I know
(without a doubt)
what
I
am*

*So
it must be you who doesn't know
and
since I do know
I don't
and
I won't
spend any more
of my time
my precious time
using your
devastating
standards
to try
to tell
you
what I am
Or
What I am not*

you
can
call me
whatever you want
you can call my fathers
shiftless
lazy
and
unconcerned

You can call my mother
a good niggah
call my son
or
daughter
illegitimate bastards
call my brother
a
pimp
a
hustler
call my sister
a whore
a prostitute
or
a
refined call girl

call me ....

I am now
beginning to
wonder
about
me

I
I think
maybe
I let you influence me
but I know what I am
you don't
so
right now
I am going to stop
spending my valuable time
using
your crazy
meaningless words

to
tell
you
what
I
am
not!!!

MISUNDERSTANDING

My mother doesn't understand me
this makes me feel so bad
a more loving child than I
a woman never had

she begs me to iron my hair
she says it will look so nice
but mommie it's not natural
I tell her once, I tell her twice

she says I shouldn't dream of Africa
because I was born right here
I feel the need of a homeland
there's nothing for her to fear

she says she's tired of black power
everywhere black this & black that
mother, I say, we need a weapon
black power is my bat

she wonders where she went wrong
I know she tried her best
with talks of love and peace
I was equipped to flunk the test

one day she'll understand
and know why I chose this way
when she finds that approaching whiteness
just
doesn't
seem
to
pay

(published in the san francisco city college newspaper 1969)

If They Come In The Morning

If they come in the morning
prepare at night they must
for if they are ever to find me
they will have to start at dusk

The night is OH so long
I'm truly tired of the wait
I know deep within
it is me they hate

I wonder why they hate me?
I've committed no crime
they've hated things I represent
since the beginning of time

if I am non-violent
then everyday I cry
little seems to work
but my heart knows why

Martin was a good man
marches of peace he led
he had the wrong approach though
now he's stone-cold dead

Angela with much education
knew what she was talking about
but now she's faced with jail
I wonder....
will she ever get out

Militancy doesn't work either
revolutionists fare 'bout as well
they get shot by the man in blue
who says "Oh what the hell"

I don't know what to do
right now I really can't say
all avenues have been traveled
and none seem to be the way

I've got to hurry and get ready
I've got to leave this place
the man creates so many problems
I hate to see his face

I don't know where I'll go
the man is everywhere
If I go to the end of time
I'm sure he'll be right there

I will strive empower myself
so no longer will I be afraid
and if they come in the morning
I will fill their souls with dread

FOOL ARE YOU

fool are you
the negro
wishing all the time
you
were
white

white with white skin
blue eyes
blond hair

white with white skin
brown eyes
brown hair

or

black hair
still white
still fool

fool are you
the negro
who must wear straight hair
who laughing call
your straight hair
or
theirs
the white girl
still white
still fool

fool are you
man who goes to war
giving blood
in white man's battle
they start the wars
you fight the battles

some of you give life
your most valuable possession
for
what?

to return
to a country
where your own kinfolk
your own dear Uncle Sam
mistreats you

fool are you
who believe
preachings of justice
of equality
a pack of lies
you know
I know
money doesn't equalize
if money doesn't

surely
black skin
and
wooly hair can't

fool are you
for believing such nonsense

fool are you
for being ashamed
of
what
you
are

you are different from all others
please remain so
stop letting the man screw you
your mind
your body
your soul
ashamed of being black

fool are you

wise are we
few in number
trying so hard to stay black
against so many negative forces
we
fight
hard
too hard

it shouldn't be necessary
to
try
so
hard

therefore my hope this day
is
for our number to increase
then
stronger
will
we
be

So

if you see me going wrong
if ever
you
see
me
going wrong
tap me on my shoulder
and say

fool
you
must
be

turning

pages

WOMAN TO WOMAN

Hey girl
before you start talking 'bout
your man
Let me tell you 'bout this guy I met

He was cool
you know
real cool
he was fine
you know
real fine

He had b-a-a-a-a-a-d rags
He wore a natural that was
oh so together
He was cool, dark and creamy
He was built strong and solid

Shit!

This niggah was
cool
super cool
bad

       super bad
   fine
       super fine

He drove a Cadillac limousine
white
       on white
in white

girl
the fenders were white gold
the keys were white gold

He talked shit
            more shit than a city sewer could collect in a whole year
365 days!

His teeth were laced
distinguishingly
with gold
white gold

This cat was cool
        super cool
                bad
                            super bad
                                fine
                                        super fine

He said he was the inventor of love
the image of peace
the perpetuator of happiness

He was freedom (he thought)

He WAS cool
        real cool
                bad
                            super bad
                                fine
                                        real fine

So

> *We went to his pad*

Ooh
IT
WAS
SLICK
Girlllllll!

> *it was white*
>> *on white*
>>> *in white*

The silverware was white gold
The ashtrays were white marble

This niggah was cool
> *super cool*
>> *bad*
>>> *super bad*
> *fine*
>> *super fine*

Girlllllll!
> *this niggah was slick*
> *this niggah talked shit*

So
I had to see

If he was cool to the bone
bad to the bone
fine to the bone

I had to see
Exactly where he was coming from

He told me he was the king
the ruler
of the universe
of the world
So
I had to see

If he was black to the bone
cool
bad
fine
to the bone

He bought me a white negligee
trimmed in white mink

Girlllll!
this niggah was cool
          real cool
               fine

                    real fine
                         bad

                              real bad

We got down
          all
               the
                    way
                         down

We got down
    On his bed
we
got
 down

white on white in white
we
got
 down

                  all the way down

This niggah and me
     this super cool
         super fine
           super bad
             niggah and me

Girl
this man was cool
real cool
fine
real fine

                bad
                  real bad

But

HE WAS A LOUSY LAY!

WHAT IT IS

A rose on a snow-white bed
   a tulip laying quietly by the side
      a kiss on the lips
         the petals shiver
            the mountains must be crossed

Fingertips caress the twig
   the twig began to drip
      twig expanding
         twig expanding
            dripping white blood

Cross the mountains
   suck the sweet tops
      in the valley
         the leaves wet and moist
            the petal is ready to burst

Lick the petal
   kiss the leaves
      taste the sweet bitterness

A thrust is coming
   slow
      gentle
         hard
            fast
               deep
                  deeper

Expand
expand
touch the walls
feel the moisture
the dampness
the sweetness
all melting together

The Pant
The Scream
The End

A beautiful flower
A beautiful twig

(1971)

INTROSPECTION

Thinking of you
As I listen to cerebral dialogue
The right hemisphere saying to the left
This love is so good!
Never before have I felt love like this!

The left hemisphere saying to the right
You hopeless romantic
A love so good is not real
Surely it can't last forever

This lover has a wife
and
a life
Of movies
Of late night pizza
Of early morning breakfast
Not to mention
Intoxicating romance

Girlfriend
please tell me
just what it is you've got
Real love?
Conversation?
Hugs?
Kisses?

No movies
No late night pizza
No early morning breakfast
Loving when convenient
or
when time allows

Since I really wasn't an invited
participant in this conversation
I WILL mind my own business
but girlfriend, just remember
thangs ain't always what they seem to be

HEARTBREAKERS

Sharing is heartbreaking
especially when that shared is
especially essential to life
especially to the essence of living

Caring is heartbreaking
when it has limits or boundaries
when it is not divided equally
because fear prohibits

Loving is heartbreaking
when not returned in full
because the one loved
is
in
love
with
another

FEELINGS

undefinable
warm and cold

tears somewhere
waiting

for
the least provocation

a memory
of
a man once loved

a memory
of
the need to love

a memory desired
of
a time when love was true

feelings of love
undefinable
warm
cold
and
indifferent

Majoniwasa Utishala

Why Cry

My dear
My darling
My love

What it is
I do not know

Love?

it cannot be
love does not exist

my hints
my clues
went wholly disregarded
acknowledge me
you nearly refused

it was you I wanted
but all the time I knew
so
it is my fault
no one else's

I have been hurt
many times before
so
I must say to myself
I
am
the
fool

if a fool gives a damn
fool
then
I
must
be

I knew of the woman
I knew of her place

but
YOU
made me believe
that
a
place
I
had
with you

a
place
I
wanted
badly
a
place
that
did
not
exist
who is sorry?
me
only

for failing
to face it
for refusing
to admit it

now

I am certain
there is no place for me
with you or anyone

I

am
alone
forever
without

Emotions Mixed

A frowned smile
dark neon lights
on bright ghetto streets
flash precariously
Darling I love You!

(I think)

Proceed with caution
Handle with care
Pushing close
Ultimate coolness
Warmed lovemaking
a tear drops

(I love)

Ramblings of Love

*Babe
still thinking of you
still feeling you*

*since
the pain
of ecstasy*

*since
the tears
of loving you*

fell

unnoticed?

maybe

*watched you dress
skin so fair
eyes so blue
or
gray
green
or
hazel you say?*

felt your skin moist
purposely
deliberately
wet
fresh
from a shower

blond hair
wet

I love you babe

prematurely

maybe

afraid
of the thought
of love
again

'cause
usually
love is
60-40
or
70-30

not the real thing
and
this will not do
so
insecure
so
afraid

endlessly rambling
trying to define feelings
got something to say

'cause

I think

I love you

afraid

feelings

premature

maybe

'cause

never in life
have I loved
one so fair
one so radiant
the sun
shining

blue eyes
blond hair
a black man
standing tall

ancestors
black
somewhere
and
white
somewhere

got much love to give
a basic need

so insecure
so unsure
I say to my self
run and pray

'cause
I don't know

'cause
I can't define
those feelings

afraid
running scared
unsure

constantly wanting
to feel the closeness
of
your touch
your breast
your neck
your ears

to taste
your kiss

feelings
enjoyed

your body
alive
deep
inside mine
ooooooooooooooh so good!

Ramblings
of
love
go
on!

(gap 10/88)

FOOL LOVE

Love is the most
    unique fool
    in the universe
because
    it has all power
and
can't use it
    has no power
and
    is strong
but

love
the most unrivaled force
    in the universe
is
    constantly working for no wages
    giving without receiving
    being mistaken for weakness

therefore

    love
    the powerful universal ruler
    is
    the
    most
    unique
    fool

LOVE

Love
is
a
four letter word
that doesn't exist
except
in
the
minds
of
those
who
are
the crazed
fanatics

Love is
hurt
and pain
and suffering
and tears
and emptiness
and loneliness
and coldness
and fear
and confusion
and disgust
and disappointment
and hate

love

is

a

four letter word

that does exist

in

the

warped

minds

of

those

who

are

the crazed

fanatics

Like Me!

I CRY

I cry
my heart cries
my soul cries

because

What I need
my heart needs
my soul needs

but

I don't have
my heart doesn't have
my soul doesn't have

why

My man
man of my heart
man of my soul
is loved
by another

Her heart cries
her soul cries
to him
to me
to us

I hear her

crying
daily
nightly

so

I cry
my heart cries
my soul cries

because

she
has him

I
can
not!

(greg)

Love Letter #1

Thoughts inspired
electrically
chemically
bring songs of an absent rhythm

calmness of inner turmoil
tears at the sunset of dust
visions of thundering and lightning
bring peace of a quiet storm

prose with promise of wandering warms

aroused by intimate moisture
with no obvious source of dew
wishing silently and praying secretly
for a womb to bear fruit once more

selectively barren past pain crazed
now desiring fair fruit from your tree
life from you to nourish inside me
a real combination of ourselves
gray eyes growing tall in your likeness

penetrating distance drawing on nearness

love
pain confused
origin deep
stiffly thrusting deeper
flying low a junkie needing more
sinking higher on a fertile corner
while blindly yearning for sight

poisoned by the closeness of touching
sweet bitterness another life to come

Ouch
dayum!
it
hurts oh
soooooooooooo good

Baby
this is all just to say

you know
I
really
really
do
love
you

(gap 82)

Love Letter #2

*My dearest friend
my love
it has appeared to me this day
the needs you have
the needs I have
can be satisfied the same way*

*My dearest friend
my love
you will be in time
'cause i'm gonna try
harder than hard
just to make you mine*

*My dearest friend
my love
problems we both have it seems
but
I promise to be in your corner
where will I make real your dreams*

*My dearest friend
my love
your **every** wish is my command
whatever you wish for
will be granted
just by the wave of your hand*

My dearest friend
my love
your happiness is my goal
happily in love we'll be
together as we grow old

(gregg 6/82)

THE WAIT

Waiting your call
body tense
almost orgasmic
nerves with endings exposed
generalized body tingling
feeling the heated moisture
of
my
being

Waiting
ecstatically
for your action and reaction
caring without limiting
ready to receive
the positive
note
you
give

Conversation in stereo
the resonance of your voice
arousing the subconscious
while numbing memories
of
past
disappointments

Waiting
deliriously
apprehensive of the strong attraction
erogenous zones encompassing me
control sublimed by the warmth
of your sincerity
& your smile

Waiting
body tense
now screaming
fervently lusting for your nearness
to engulf me in your aura
to permit coitus
in the opiate of your manhood

I wait
come
please
come
close
and
bring
me
with
you

drown me in your wetness
revive me with your passion

(alfred /feb 1985)

LOVE NOTES

With the urge to scribble fleeting thoughts
legibly I write
prose
poetic verse absent
there's no need for annotated response

again hoping
(not waiting)
for your call

telephone rings
body screams
deep stabbing awakening
of
subconscious fantasy
dayum!
right number
wrong body

deciding while waiting
4 u 2 need me
i've "got to put things in perspective"
(that's what my momma say)
"girlllllllll put goochi dust in his bread"
the voodoo priestess says
"put the juice of menses in his soup"
suggested the Nigerian medicine man

instead patiently I wait
for my name or my number
to
move
up
on your list
of
priorities

feelings
still no way forgotten
the clasp of your hand
warm in mine
an automatic gesture
that went unnoticed by you

wondering occasionally
if you even know my name
know yours well
I say it often
(during moments of dreamed ecstasy)

attempting contentment
'cause you've forgotten that I am
when you looked at me I saw you

don't know what I saw you see
'cause your subdued expression I couldn't read
interpretation needed
patience IS a virtue

Longing for a time
to be close and fondle
your nose
your ears
your beard
feeling the heat of delayed penetration

Lying in your arms
on your chest

whispering empty conversation
a love junkie
getting high on your voice
while breathing in your space

adding to your existence
subtracting doubts and insecurities
becoming tremorous with your nearness
while loving you
as
allowed

(alfred 2/25/83)

For You My Love

*My Darling this day
with reference to the cliche
"A bird
in the hand
is worth
two in the bush"*

*I want you to know
I would gladly sacrifice
the bird
my right hand
and
the two in the bush
for
you*

02/28/83

REALITY

I love you deeply
tried my damnedest
to let you know

acknowledgment you refuse
of
what you know is true

realizing all the time
i'm just a name on your list
another number in your book

pain is now my intimate companion

of my destiny
no longer am I sure
perhaps
it
is

to be alone
heartbroken
missing you

(1971)

LIFE

*There was a time
when all thoughts
of you and me
were so neatly packaged
and placed on a shelf*

*There was a time
when enchanting memories
of moments together
were so neatly packaged
and placed on a shelf*

*There was a time
when I was pretty dayum sure
that thoughts and memories
packaged and shelved
would remain forever unmoved*

*SUDDENLY
without warning
you re-entered my life
tore open the packages
knocked down the shelves*

*and
now
I am
thoroughly
confused*

(Otis 3/83)

Majoniwasa Utishala

AGAIN IN RETRO

Thinking of
past conversations
filled with
unvoiced desires
theoretical promises
and
what-if philosophies

wondering why contentment
no longer is found
in the noisy televised companionship
of
late late shows

needing to feel
the warmth of your body
marvel in the richness of your color
as we relax in the perfect peace
of our exhaustion

yearning
for satisfaction
received from your nearness
touching you at will
while tracing your silhouette in the darkness

tearfully fearing the release
of protected emotions
unleashed by the strength
and reality of our oneness

enjoying the rhythm
played by your respirations
painfully tolerating engorgement

a true indication
of
needs
not
met

(alfred 04/05/83)

Majoniwasa Utishala

MEMOIR

just a few lines
to let you know
our closeness
was truly enjoyed

re-kindled flames
in a dusty
cob-webbed fireplace
re-minded me
that
we
were

at will
you re-entered my life
a night of loving
a moment blessed
&
you're gone

re-minded me
of days gone by
when we came easily
reciprocated
&
endeared

as you departed
my mind refused question
but from a hidden void
my soul cried an answer

WE LOVE!

(Otis 3/83)

TEARS

Tears from deep within
a well
overflowing
a dam
barrier broken
a river
overtaking the body

of a heart
that is scared to define

feelings
uncertain
because
it
may
be
love
again

Majoniwasa Utishala

REGROUPINGS

as a pebble gently tossed to sea
ripples forever 'til infinity

like the disrupted peace
of a quiet storm
my space
is
re-entered by you

a purposeful endeavor
shock therapy self-inflicted
a desperate attempt
to
regain lost composure

re-shaping my life
mesmerized by your re-entry
alive with desire
overflowing with passion
amid new-found confusion

mourning your departure
loathing our distance
and
spiritually traveling with you
on
the starship love

(Otis 3/83)

REFLECTIONS

This day finds me
making feeble attempts
to restore my soul
re-package my life
and re-shelf my emotions

with every breath
of every awakened moment
your image appears
an ebon statue
of gleaming perspiration
kneeling above and within me

formed unformed thoughts
bringing into focus
unforgotten perception
probably misplaced agony
of the temporary inability
to get it all

the screaming pant of orgasm
following the deep penetration of your maleness
often mistaken for pain
a tantalizing revival
of a woman re-made

soooooooo

This day finds me
spending much energy
trying so hard
to send vivid memories
of your nearness
deep into my subconscious

(Otis 03/06/83)

LOVER PLEASE

man in life of woman
loved deep with rare repayment
desires not to love but to fuck
as dictated by libido

lover of all seasons
buying milk
or
bread when needed

a shoulder to cry on
or
an ear to listen to life-related bullshit

main man
be a lover at all times
not only when convenient
or
when the need arises

love me without interruption
remember to want me
for the same reasons I want you
feel the closeness
the singular heat of our existence
without paranoia strengthened by fear
of sensual captivity

false securities found
excuses made for not belonging
simply because
you
don't want
me
to want
you

blame society
blame environmental factors
for
failing miserably to properly sequence priorities

please
do not
invent reasons for excuses
or
legitimize excuses for reasons
'cause
i've made the decision
to love you
to bewitch you
to remove your fears & insecurities
to complete my fantasy
to convert to true love

that we may live
together
in
love
forever

IMAGERY

Hours spent looking
photo misplaced
from sight protectively hidden

enhancing my trip
conquering the distance
through space and time
we're apart

photo found
aids transcension
we visit your place and mine

vivid color
a live reproduction
appreciated opportunity
of holding you near

from organic imagery
cosmic contentment
imprinted in mind
reprinted on paper
always
I
love

(Otis 3/83)

LOVE ENCOUNTERS

quietly screaming
ALIVE FOREVER
while earnestly attempting
to recapture a moment physically gone

savoring the aroma of your cologne
blended well with natural oils
my body is touched by yours

intoxicated by your presence
spellbound by the warmth of your breath
mindlessly listening to the rhythmic peace
of your respirations

fearing the inevitable sexual encounter
wet with neurotic anticipation
my body prepares to receive yours
I marvel at my response

reveling in the moisture of our oneness
enjoyment heightened by your whisper
oooooooooooohhh
GIRL I LOVE YOU SOOOOOOOO MUCH

I sense a need
only
to love
you more!

(alfred 5/6/83)

TIME SPENT

Thinking of you
I SPEND TIME
reflecting on touching you
feeling your wetness

Trying to decide
I SPEND TIME
where, darling, do we go from here
friends and lovers we'll always be

Wondering about you
I SPEND TIME
re-listening to expressed anxieties
wishing they'd all disappear

Wanting to re-assure you
I SPEND TIME
hoping you understand that
my only purpose is to enhance your life

Missing you
I SPEND TIME
wanting to be certain that you know
that
I
care

(alfred 04/83)

LOVER'S PRAYER

My Dearest Darling, My Love

My prayer this day
is to be close to you
to touch your soul
to be held in your arms
and make love to you

My prayer this day
is to be close to you
to taste the sweetness
of your flesh
to make love to you

My prayer this day
is to be close to you
to receive the fullness of your manhood
while making love to you

My prayer this day
is to be close to you
to be soothed by the coolness of the evaporation
of your perspiration
after making love to you

My prayer this day
is to be close to you
to enjoy the peaceful sleep
of total sexual gratification
only to wake up
and
make love to you
again

(alfred 6/8/83)

CONTEMPLATIONS

My dearest darling, my love
I sit here
trying hard to determine
just where we go from here

My dearest darling, my love
I sit here
thanking you
for allowing me
to
be
close

My dearest darling, my love
I sit here
asking myself
if the taste of honey you gave
was just a taste

My dearest darling, my love
I sit here
wondering if indeed
I have erred

I
have
erred
but
only
by
loving you

too
much

My dearest darling, my love
I sit here
desiring eternal unity
hoping to be an integral part
of
your
life

My dearest darling, my love
I sit here
resolving this day
not to put me so far out front
and
allow you
to
love
me
if
you
will

(alfred 5/11/83)

THANK YOU DARLING

I say
thank you darling
knowing fully that "thank you"
is an inexpensive
and cowardly way
of saying things
that so badly need to be said

I say
thank you darling
for allowing me to be me
for allowing me to love you
for being receptive of my shortcomings
for understanding my insecurities

I say
thank you darling
for walking in the park
for kissing in the dark
for permitting me to relax
in your arms

I say
thank you darling
for enhancing my life
for supporting my endeavors
for giving me a place
deep within your space

I say thank you darling
for the stimuli you give
for the daily encouragement to excel
for overlooking my imperfections
for making my dreams and fantasies real

I say
thank you darling
for awakening sleeping emotions
for rescuing me from drowning
in self-programmed despair
for loving me as you do

oblivious of repetition
for all said and done

gratefully
and
simply
I say

thank you darling!

(alfred 6/08/83)

Majoniwasa Utishala

CORRESPONDENCE *(Unspoken)*

just had to send you a line or two
prose with poetic edges
a note to the one loved
a written message of non-verbal thanks

Man standing tall and serene
acutely complexioned with ebon coloring
a quick glance at timepiece
a prayer to father time and mother nature

accepting the mystery of the on-coming night
oblivious of our impromptu meeting
desirous of episodic fulfillment
        of life lived in available zones

not gonna measure energy levels lost
to my emotional turbulence
'cause le rendezvous now depleted
began with so much more

running scared
        out of control

non-verbal thanks for dimensions restored
apologizing for fiery moments
that occurred as a result of transferring energy
from
your
space
to
mine

(Otis 7/83)

DEAREST DARLING

thinking of you
getting high on the thoughts

relishing the sweet bitterness
that comes with the moisture of your kiss

soaring on flashbacks
of time spent together

dearest darling
*   WE LOVE*

(otis 4/25/84)

SILHOUETTE

living silhouette of ebon color
shimmering nude blackness
distinguishing facial lines
reminiscent of African heritage
clothed fashionably in American culture

hearing the mystique in your voice
filling a non-existent void
with philosophical discussion
and unanswerable questions

heated moisture of a kiss
simmering storm revived
fear of engulfing passion
keep excited bodies apart

luster of a starlit night
dimmed by unfulfilled desire
chills warmed by being close
while dancing to the silent beat
of a slow song

touching deliberately and carefully
denying agitation or arousal
emotions agonizingly restrained
by merciless demands of daily living

(otis 1985)

WAITING

Counting the seconds
    of the hours of the day
        seems like a lifetime

weak with anticipation
    of your homecoming

preparing to greet you
    with shower
        make up
            and cologne

special efforts made to keep you
    alive with wonder and fascination
    body clothed scantily (American style)
    attempting to arouse your fantasy

perfumed chest
    rhythm of a beating heart confused
    by the musk of a work day gone
    and
the salty residue of perspiration on your cheek

excitement triggered
by the sound of your voice
flowing easy with disconnected re-accounts
empty conversation perpetuated by nearness
increasing chatter turning me on

(3/16)

LOOKING AT YOU

when looking at you
I fall on my knees
pray to god all powerful
I thank him for a man
who loves me as much
as I love him

when looking at you
I wonder why
you have no equipment to protect
your eyes and your body
from the ultraviolet light
of my existence
an obvious effect
symbolizing
the transformation
of being in love

when looking at you
a smile is summoned
an eruption
bubbling from within
a ticket for admission
to an asylum
for the emotionally insane

when looking at you
my body screams
remembering
recently passed times
of sharing life
of hugging and kissing
of loving and caring
and being close

when looking at you
fear overwhelms me
as I force withdrawal
from the society
of imperfect love

when looking at you
cautiously I move
toward renewed interest
and silently I question
realities to come

(benny 2/86)

FOR BENNY

This is for you Benny
for the evening
I thank you
for the monotony you broke
for charming me
with
endless
resonant
conversation

the issues discussed
of your ex
of my ex
of your children
and
mine

the worldly needs
of ambition-less youth
of babies having babies
supported by the county

back

to the issue at hand
to you and me
to me and you
a perfect unforced fit

but

if my subdued or not subdued
aggression made you uneasy
so
be
it
I
apologize

if the moisture
of an unpredicted kiss
stolen during a scene
in the movie
"The Color Purple"
chilled you to the bone
please be advised
the need for the steal
chilled
me
first

leaning a dazed head on your shoulder
pretending absorption in the movie
enjoying the comfort
of
your
nearness
anticipation mounting
remembering comments
          and
questions shared
surreptitiously
in passing

(Feb 1986)

I chose not to reveal
the amount of time
you spent in my dreams
or
the mission you fulfilled

I say only that upon awakening
I kissed the place on my pillow
where
you slept
so peacefully

afraid to open my eyes
fearful of reassurance
perhaps
that piece of my night
was
not
real at all

awaiting the day
of the dream come true
awake after midnight
looking at your sleeping face
on my pillow
as my body screams
good morning my love!

sleepless dream

sleepless midnight calm
broken by disconcerted televised noises
of pre-learned lines
ineffectively babbled
unsolicited entertainment
a challenging struggle to define
the undeveloped plot
of an out-dated black and white movie

loverless
selectively unaccompanied
body chilled
unemotionally warmed
by a blanket of electrically heated coils
temperature determined by Westinghouse
an impotent substitute for the natural warmth
generated by a body in heat

speechless patronizing mirror
nonchalantly watching
independently observing
thoughtless
unorganized arrangement
of multi-colored rollers
in recently permed hair

dreamless reproductions of past conversation
satisfaction of time spent with lovers remembered
performance relished
wishing for instant replay
while desperately attempting
to summon missed relaxation
of
ecstatically exhausted sleep

(earl 1988)

LOVE LETTER #3

Prose seeping from my well
of injured emotions
love letter written
an answer to the invisible
"Dear John"

in my dreams entertainment uncanny
the scent of your cologne
the softness of your skin
yet unknown

weeks passing
pinching myself
a concerted effort
to convince me
that
love
and
life
are real

promising between pinches
to talk more
trust more
love without inhibitions
hoping that
my chance for love
has finally come
a beautiful evening
unruffled by the rock band
of a ghetto club
weary of freedom

of unbridled expression
of heightened desire to please

Reliving the warm calmness
while capturing miles of freeway
nodding and sleeping in love
with a promise of forever together
unless
bored and overwhelmed
by daily living routines
and the monotony
*   of*
* missionaries making love*
or
unplanned excitement
shared senility
and helpless thoughts
of
past sexual encounters

dreams changed to nightmares
introduced by false contentment
enforced restless patience
jumping at phone bells
teased by wrong numbers

uuuuuummm
where does love go
*   when it's gone*

body integrity mutilated
by constant conversation
while never-ending memories
undoubtedly set the mood
for
tears
to
come

in my head
I hear your laughter
I am aroused by its sound
in search of you
I scrutinize dark images
hoping that you'll materialize
to convince me again
that
love
is!

(benny 2/86)

uncertain reality

recapturing events of days gone by
body made tremorous by your nearness
aroused by mental replays
involuntarily reliving your moves

questioning life's existence without you
certain that somehow it could not have been
hopeless attempts to maintain perspective
realizing that time does really change things

scared senseless yet yearning for closeness
buried and hidden sensations revived
flower once dry in hairy jungle
suddenly moistened by an internal stream

a brief gaze into time summons your appearance
standing tall/erect
clothed/unclothed
an uncertain reality of your existence

of the imagination just a figment
body integrity lost

(michael 12/87)

DISSOLUTION

Alone in bed
> *in the front room of a house*
>> *my house*
> *owned by me and my mortgage co.*

Waiting for husband #3
> *asleep in bed in the master bedroom*
>> *of a house*
>>> *my house*
> *owned by me and my mortgage co.*

Diminishing patience
> *marriage ended*
> *no remorse*
> *no regrets*
> *relieved not unhappy*

For husband #3
> *has to find another bed*
> *in a room in a house*
> *his house*
> *owned by him and his mortgage co.*

Now wondering
if I ever have been in love
> *'cause it HAS been suggested*
that in love
> *I have not been*

'Cause not ever have I loved anyone
as much as
I
love
ME

Thinking of other women
        who at all costs
        must have a man next to them
        in a bed of a house
        owned by them and their mortgage co.

Women who have invariably stopped
        being themselves
        loving themselves
women who have
        forsaken their identity
        given up a life of contentment
        sacrificed their happiness
        to become Mr. So-N-So's wife

Maybe in the next life during a fit
        of excruciating loneliness
or
        devastating alone ness

I will pray to Allah

or
call on Ouija
  or
visit a tarot

Maybe in the next life
     I will petition for a sneak preview
     into a crystal ball or spread of cards
     in a final effort to find
that non-existent lover
to love and cherish
as husband & wife
in a house owned by us
and our mortgage co.
Until by death
do we part

(1988)

Bothered & Restless

*Bothered & restless
my pen
is again called to
dauntless prose
wicked unfulfilling
source of satisfaction*

*Bothered & restless
strained anticipation
caught in limbo
of not knowing
what awaits*

*Bothered & restless
anxiety increasing
desperately hoping
with sincere desire
all is well*

*Bothered & restless
listening to moments
tick blasphemingly away
with no sighted relief
while awaiting resolution*

*Bothered & restless
empty re-assurance
audio/visual
hearing/seeing*

MY WORLD STANDS STILL

(Jan 1988)

THIS ONE IS FOR YOU PAUL

This one is for you Paul
again called to poetic prose
effortlessly capturing untamed magic
stars shimmering
summoned abruptly
from heaven
glittering reflections
a recollection of
enchanted moments together

fleeting shadows (of) shared romanticism
huggingly pulled tightly into your aura
erasing the pangs of acute desire
aching with knowledge of cool awareness

daily waking to suspicions of missed dreams
engulfed by sensations of ecstatic fulfillment
now regrettably haunted by the need to feel you
enviously knowing that you are where
I should have been

you resuming the past
me desiring the present
re-incarnated Paul the III
same familiar fairness
height and gentleness
a mental reference
friend/lover returned

this one is for you Paul

guilty only of
rushed friendship
and
unpremeditated lovemaking
thanking you for complete contentment
uncertain definitions
of emotional statements
in near total disregard
of
who
you
really
are

(09/26/88)

EXCERPTS FROM MIXED EMOTIONS

Feelings
sort of
I owe you
an apology
an A P O L O G Y

sort of
sort of

the last encounter
enjoyed a lot
enjoyed a lot

Im promp tu
may or may not be the word
the word
your word

Encounter enjoyed
encounter enjoyed
like Momma's potato pie
a hunger and need for more
(did try to eat it all up once)

you are
blushing
blushing
cover your face

I am embarrassed
I feel your cheeks
hot
hot
blushing
blushing

irresponsible?
ir re spon si ble!
Your word
your word
but
I will take the irresponsible rap

didn't mean to be
ir re spon si ble
impromptu
your word
your word

if you were offended in any way
while sharing a bottle of tequila
I a po lo gize

by

by whatever means necessary
or
by whatever turns you on

darling
I apologize

I a po lo gize
while
asking
for an encore
what can we do

(paul 1988)

BACK IN LOVE AGAIN

Body enveloping embrace
smoldered flames ignited
by heated wetness of a tongued kiss
resistance fleeting restrain failing

Soul in discord - heart in turmoil
desperately attempting to regain composure
waning control potential explosion
of volcanic activity unleashed

pleasure of multiple orgasms achieved
whispered confusion utterance clarified
unpolled question silently answered
by actions that say much more than words

(Feb 1998)

FIREPLACE SAGA

Sitting here in delirium
caused by unquenched desires
resulting from the inability
to recapture
your voice
your smile
and
your touch

watching flames
dancing angrily
in disconcerted rebellion
to the fuel
of a fire
not lit by you

vividly recollecting
an enchanted occasion
the last fireplace fire
with flames
so effortlessly
kindled by you

hearing unrehearsed crackles
of a duet chaotically song
(by) confined flames
joined by the screeching hum
of a
hostile smoke alarm

a song with the main chorus absent
me singing your name
a suppressed outward expression
orgasm internalized

rainbow-colored flames
splash-painting your name
in multi-dimensional letters
framed
by fireplace-blackened bricks

engulfed by warmth
emanating from
flames dancing passionately
re-assuring me
that
times passed
will
come
again

(paul 11/88)

LOVE LETTER #4

Lying here feeling criminal
refusing serious thought
wondering if this cloud
(the one you've put me on)
is really mine for keeps
or
am I just an unwitting accomplice
to the crime
of
stealing clouds from the sky

subduing tears
of overwhelming elation
your kiss
involuntarily solicited
while yearning for the tease
of a candlelit dance
to a slow song

body
hypnotized
mesmerized
relenting to total seduction
transcendentally feeling and seeing you
awake asleep
smiling
solemn
clothed/unclothed
miraged image
an oasis in my mind
video-ed reproduction

shadows on parade
in the flameless fire
of the fireplace

promised indulgence
in already-purchased Asti
unleased pent-up inhibitions
relaxing in jets of a whirl-pooled bath
grooving to the motion
of
motorized jet-streamed currents
while making love in the heated bubbles
of water-driven cradle
that
promises me
and
promises you

that this chapter
will
be
continued

(paul 10/88)

OUT OF CONTROL

Hurting from head to toe
inside and outside
tears of disappointment and contempt
refusing to flow

wondering how that which feels so good
can turn around and hurt so bad
was it something I did
or
was it something I said

were energies and lovemaking
shared real
or
imagined
or
just something to pass time
to satisfy your male ego
to relax the erect
or
simply pacify your libido

disgusted with myself
for allowing you
to set up house
inside my love

forgotten in the heat of passion
that fate has promised
fulfillment so complete
is not for me

not in this life
not in the next

so

today I promise me
to forever maintain an aloofness
never again allowing intimate sharing
and
just in case the irrepressible need arises
I will follow the suggestion
of the artist 'formally known as Prince'
and
do it with a magazine!

(paul 10/88)

WINNINGS (NEXT LIFE)

Thinking of you
madly searching for the anchor
a desperate attempt to debark
to put an end to the cruise
on the boat going nowhere

How often
          if ever
do you allow yourself
thoughts of your impact
on my life

Long hours awake
nights without sleep
talking to myself
amused by
Super Mario Brothers III
sent from heaven
in a sarcastic response

Extra time spent
in six to eight hour extensions
placed on the end
of an 8 to 5

Silent prayers unanswered
Dear Nintendo I thank you

hushed wish for
a lotto bowl
or
a bingo bowl

this IS the next life
my number was chosen

my prize
a life-time endowment
of
hugging
&
kissing
of
conversation
&
warmth

saying no is no longer an option

loving you so
reminiscence of days of love gone by
ruefully joining Sam Cook in the background
soulfully singing 'Darling You Send Me'

infatuation
imageless reflection
emotions anesthetized!

(geary 3/90)

THIS IS NOT A LOVE LETTER THIS ONE IS FOR YOU PAUL

and no!

hell no!

It is NOT just another love letter

emotions demanding prose poetic
or
prose not quite poetic

it is a written
articulated
reminder

that

feelings
have not changed

cold sweats & palpitations continue
at the thought of you
at the sight of you
at hearing someone call your name

this one is for you Paul
a love letter

damn

maybe
to say simply

that

feelings are real
and
remain constant

this one IS for you Paul
just a simple reminder
that you are missed

and

out of sight

is not necessarily

out of mind

pleaded solicitation for destiny to answer
what's there for you & me
what's there for me & you

conceivably

we'll be together

in another place
or
at another time???

(paul 12/89)

WHY ME?

(am I the keeper of your insecurities)

There are many questions
there may not be answers to
why me?
why me?
why me?

Is it because I've worked so hard
to get where I am today
maybe I would be better off
a broken down ghetto welfare queen
with numerous babies' daddies
and the MENtality to match

feelings of inadequacy
maybe then would not surface
because
you
Mr. John Doe Black Man
in some thwarted genocidal way
could then feel superior

to me

if I had not a decent place to live
if I had not a sports car to drive
if I had not a salaried job
perhaps then
could you find a place for me in your heart

perhaps then
you could love me just a little
and find comfort and security in knowing
that my peace
my happiness
my livelihood
rest squarely on your shoulders
and
permit you to be
the man you think you are

maybe then you could
maybe then you would
find the very basic personal security
find the very basic personal security
that would enable you
to feel less threatened by me
that would enable you to realize
that
my
pseudoprosperity
can
potentially

provide
a less stressful life
for both
you
and
for me!

(2000)

FALLING

Hopeless attempt to 'get a grip'
lady in leather
or
shimmering panty hose
psyche in discord
heart in turmoil
waning out of control
explosion potential
catalytic activity unleased

encompassing embrace
failed suppression
resistance leaving
embers re-ignited
oxygen depleted
by a tongued kiss

unpoised questions
answered/unanswered
pleasured organization achieved
muffled mumbling clarified
thank you darling so very very much

(April 1998)

HUMMMMMM (DAYDREAMING)

sometimes wishing you were deep within
my essence
my ambiance
the slap of destiny made me a one-man woman
you were the one man
apologies may be in order
prematurely perhaps
physical
mental
emotional drain
understanding the smile
and
the reason why
an earnest attempt
to be void of previous rhetoric
of love
and
of lovers lost
while the stale aroma of your cologne
remaining in my pores
remaining in my clothing
a constant reminder
that
we
were

turning pages

CELEBRATE LIFE

celebrate the lives of those whose blood runs through our veins
some of whom we don't even know
with every breath
celebrate death and dying
'cause for everyone
everyday
is one less

remember the grandmother or grandfather
mother or father
husband or wife
uncle or aunt
sister or brother
niece or nephew
cousin
child
or the in-law that mingled and produced

remembering brings
smiles sometimes
and
tears sometimes
and
sometimes
just a reflection on the what-ifs

what if . . .
instead of finding Viagra
the REAL Fountain of Youth had been found
and
50 was the magic number
aging stopped after that
"Momma-Dear ... I can't believe you are ... uuuuuummmm ...
you don't look a day over 40"

what if . . .
wars and disagreements were settled on the dance floor
and
bullet was just a name for the latest dance step
or
the money spent on the last space mission
was used to cure cancer, emphysema or AIDS

what if . . .
grandmother or grandfather
mother or father
husband or wife
uncle or aunt
sister or brother
niece or nephew
cousin
child
or the in-law that mingled and produced
was still here with me (or you)

but
because
of
the fun we shared
the love we shared
the tears we shared
or the words we never had to speak

and

because
of
the life we took part in
and
the things it taught us
with a simple touch
of
the mind
the body
or
the soul

those who have gone on before us were friends not just relatives

and
because life CAN go on
without those dearly beloved and departed

and

although I KNOW the past cannot be re-created
(except in my mind)
when I remember
I smile sometimes
I cry sometimes

and

selfishly wish they were here

August 3, 2002
for the wilson family reunion

turning

pages

MISDEMEANOR

Vet'N'Red synonym for lear jet
an unidentified flying object
appearing out of nowhere
cruisin' the interstate
in preparation of weekend celebration

packaged confusion of never ending road
fervent quest for emotional calm
a Ford pick-up or UFO?
Search interrupted by a welcomed sighting
point of origin unknown
misdemeanor or shameless coincidence
off-ramp on-ramp lost found
jammed disjointed highways
combined by bright lights and neons
of traffic-ed city streets

Cordial uninhibited dialogue
late night meeting arranged
Jamaican party in the ghetto
reggae for you new experience for me
Climax unorchestrated
libido satisfied

Elayne Anderson

RAILROAD TRACKS

wandering through the city
stereo blasting soul music
my sports car shiny brand new
hair do-ed every strand in place
sculptured nails enameled fire red
body clothed in Nordstrom's finest

women and children are seen
wretched bewildered anguished
hidden between walls under roofs
men and boys cornrows unruly with wear
jheri-ed curls with juice drippin'
fruitlessly attempting to recapture jheri

sable populated chocolate suburb
a place my children won't live
fragmented snapshots of city life
photos unfinished mentally framed
panorama of graffiti colored buildings
a reminder of undeveloped stories not told

turning pages

THE DAY MY MOTHER DIED
I BURIED HER

unwritten mental pronouncement
not defined by the stiffness of rigor
nor the cessation of a beating heart
yet the time for interment has come

The day my mother died I buried her

weary of the corpseless procession
reminiscent of a well-rehearsed drill team
led by calculated lies and half-truths
advancing steadily thru my life

The day my mother died I buried her

without a funeralized celebration
dignified by tearless shrouded mourners
waltzing around a coffin singing
"Oh When the Saints Go Marchin In"

The day my mother died I buried her

ears closed to obituated bullshit
of clueless apologetic well-wishers
talking about a loving person
whom they never even knew

The day my mother died I buried her

no flower-covered satin-filled casket
of decorated refinished lumber
adorning a church or parlor
dimly lit by rose-colored lamps

The day my mother died I buried her

role of child-parent resigned
and penurious servitude terminated
freedom from night-mared dreams
of
washing machines
ironing boards
and
hot stoves

The day my mother died I buried her

put on my red silk dress
my high-heeled sneakers
a sprayed mist of cologne
and
enjoyed a night on the town

(Sept 1994)

turning

pages

African Chief

you came to dinner
in my house
you dined

soul food
you tasted
you liked
you stayed

with every passing day
disappointment haunts me
Being Black in America
reading the book is hard
confusing are the pictures

pictures that change just a little
just a little do they change
but
the frame
the picture frame ... it remains the same

my people
seduced by a child of the original molesterer
sperm traded for trinkets
your seed you planted in caucasian ground
you damned the blood

the blood of MY grandfathers
dammed ... contaminated
AGAIN

history
oops
(was that) a temporary lapse ???
that WAS a temporary lapse
HIS story (I meant to say)

perhaps you never knew
as the ships crossed the ocean
OUR story changed

who are you?
WHO ARE YOU?
a visitor?
from the motherland?
or just a displaced
disoriented
green-carded
naturalized
dashiki-wearing ameriCan

(08/25/03)

the drums (they be calling me)

rhapsody from afar
leftovers . . . maybe
maybe
from a past life
where my soul slumbered
& slept through generations
now frenzied awakening
no longer able to sleep
restless disquieted stirring
spirit haunted dreams
drums and wordless chants
drums in urgent staccato
calling forth that which defies death
begging the warrior in me
the wife of the voodoo priest
to levitate to the wings of Sankofa
tripping . . . tripping
to the motherland
to participate in ceremonial communion
with ancestors
kings
queens
tribal leaders

stirring
awakening
calling
begging
defying
levitating
tripping . . . tripping

the drums
the chants
the drums
wordless chants
the drums
the drums
I
hear
drums
I
hear
chants . . . wordless
the drums
the drums
my ancestors
the tribal leaders
they
be
calling
me

(completed 05/30/03)

144